Book 7

Mmm, I Like!

by Wiley Blevins
Illustrated by Vincent Andriani

SCHOLASTIC

I like  music .

2

I like the .

monkey

3

I like the .

mirror

I like the  .

merry-go-round

I like the  .

moon

6

I like . Mmmm!

milk

My Words

and	see
does	she
he	the
hello	up
I	will
like	

Books 1–7